ATHENS
Georgia's Columned City

PHOTOGRAPHS

BY

KENNETH FREDERICK MARSH

COMMENTARY

BY

BLANCHE MARSH

ATLANTA

Cherokee Publishing Company

1979

Originally Published
Asheville, N.C., 1964

REVISED EDITION
With Addendum, 1979

Library of Congress Catalog Card Number: 79-55550
International Standard Booksellers Number: 0-87797-048-3

Copies of *ATHENS Georgia's Columned City* may be obtained through leading booksellers everywhere or by ordering direct from Cherokee Publishing Company's sales office: P.O. Box 1081, Covington, Georgia 30209. Send $5.95 plus 60¢ postage and, where applicable, Georgia Sales Tax (18¢) and Local Option Tax (6¢).

PRINTED IN THE UNITED STATES OF AMERICA

Acknowledgements

ALL TOO SOON old buildings like elusive memories disappear into the past. We hope this pictorial study of the historic structures of Athens, Georgia, will aid in the preservation of these tangible symbols of its passing years. The commentary accompanying the photographs is intended to place the buildings in their historic context.

Our mountain neighbors, Dorothy and Glenn Tucker, knowing of our interest in such projects and the beauty of Classic homes, directed us to Athens. Elizabeth Todd, Professor Emeritus, and Dolores Artau, Administrative Assistant, both of the University of Georgia, gave unstinting guidance and assistance without which the project would not have been completed.

It is not possible to mention all the good people of Athens who entered so wholeheartedly into this study. We particularly appreciate the valuable information Mrs. Howell Cobb Erwin, Sr. gave about the illustrious Cobb family. Mrs. Bradbury Foss and Mrs. Robert Segrest also have our appreciation for their furtherance of our endeavors. Professor Hubert B. Owens, head of the Department of Landscape Architecture, gave us many suggestions along with the loan of Early Architecture of Georgia by Frederick Doveton Nichols and Francis Benjamin Johnston as well as The Garden History of Georgia by Loraine M. Cooney.

The Georgiana Collection of the University of Georgia Library made available its extensive files and publications pertaining to Athens, including Annals of Athens, 1801-1901 by A. L. Hull, Sketches of Athens, 1801-1825 by Dr. Henry Hull, and Reminiscences of Athens by Edward B. Mell. Ellis Merton Coulter's book, College Life in the Old South, gave us background understanding of Athens and the University.

Our deepest gratitude goes to Mrs. James R. Warren, a past president of the Athens Historical Society, for the many hours she spent sharing her research findings and assisting us in making the commentary as accurate as possible. We owe special thanks to our friend, Jeannette C. Dennis, for her patient work in the technical preparation of this book and to the Rem Studio for the photograph of the commencement procession.

It has been a satisfaction to share with Athens this look into her proud and illustrious past.

Classic beauty in Athens—Alpha Gamma Delta Portico

Athens

Just below the foot hills of the Blue Ridge Mountains, near the confluence of the Middle Oconee and the North Oconee Rivers, lies the city of Athens amid the rolling, red clay hills of North Georgia. There, on land once owned by Daniel Easley, a city and a university grew into a center of culture and wealth, nurturing men and ideas that commanded the attention of the nation.

By 1800, a tiny settlement, not yet named Athens, had begun at Cedar Shoals where the old Cherokee Indian trader trail crossed the "clear waters" of the Oconee River. Early settlers observing student classes under the trees on the hill overlooking the river in 1801, were witnessing the beginnings of the first college west of the Savannah River. As fine Federal homes began to appear around the new campus, the role of Athens as the cultural center of Georgia became increasingly evident.

Prosperity came to the village in the 1830's as the growing of tobacco gave way to cotton in North Georgia. The cultured social life surrounding the college attracted prominent families of wealth and men of national stature who built impressive Greek Revival homes along the new streets. Three decades of ante-bellum opulence gave Athens its grand mansions with their massive columns, magnolia shaded formal gardens, and the gracious, unhurried way of life enjoyed by the planter class of the Old South.

The War Between the States interrupted the "good life" of Athens. However, under the direction of the University and such men as Benjamin Harvey Hill, Howell Cobb, and Joseph Henry Lumpkin, Athens soon resumed its growth and leadership. Devotion to the Classic in architecture continued throughout the 19th century unperturbed by street paving, gas lights, electricity, and the rest of the nation's turn to Victorian architecture.

Present day Athens still cherishes its venerable campus buildings and historic mansions where many "firsts" of the nation originated. The story of these old structures spells out highlights in the history of Georgia's columned city.

THE ARCH
1858
Entrance to Campus

Athens, the home of the University of Georgia, was appropriately named for ancient Athens, the City of Athena, Goddess of Wisdom. *The Arch* leading to the campus is modeled after the Great Seal of Georgia and its columns represent wisdom, justice, and moderation. It has been a long standing tradition that no freshman may pass through *The Arch;* presumably freshmen have yet to attain both wisdom and moderation.

The Academic Building, seen through *The Arch,* was so named in 1903 when the 1831 Ivy Building and the 1859 Library were remodeled and joined with the impressive Corinthian columns and open stairways.

OLD COLLEGE
1801-1805

Both Athens and the University of Georgia, later called Franklin College, came into being in 1801. Largely through the efforts of Abraham Baldwin, a Yale graduate, Georgia was the first state to charter a university in 1785. However, it was sixteen long years before classes started. In 1801 a committee of five men selected the site for the University on 633 acres of land donated by Governor Milledge near the Cedar Shoals, and named the spot Athens. That same year Abraham Baldwin, who had been named president of the University, took office as United States senator and resigned the presidency. Josiah Meigs, also of Yale, became the first actual president.

Old College with its bright Flemish bond brickwork was patterned after Connecticut Hall at Yale. It was the first permanent building erected on the campus. Prior to its completion, some classes were held under the trees.

It is a tradition that during the era of slavery students brought their body servants to college with them. Tiny cubicles were contrived for their quarters by partitioning off a section of the large sleeping rooms in the *Old College*. The building has served the University in various capacities from dormitory to classrooms.

Visible on the north face of *Old College* is a plaque denoting the room occupied by roommates Alexander H. Stephens and Crawford W. Long in 1832.

WADDEL HALL
1821

Waddel Hall, the second oldest permanent building on the campus, was first named Philosophical Hall. It was later named for Dr. Moses Waddel, the fifth president of the college. Through his efforts the college was saved "from languishing into despair" and the enrollment built up from 7 students in 1818 to 120 in 1821. After his resignation in 1829, he returned to Willington, South Carolina, where he had previously organized and taught at a preparatory school having John C. Calhoun as one of his pupils.

DEMOSTHENIAN HALL
1824

Two years after the college was opened, the Demosthenian Literary Society, a debating club, was founded. Such debating societies threshed out the issues of growing America. Young men, destined to become national leaders, developed their oratorical abilities in these halls of debate. It was here that the fiery Robert Toombs, United States Senator, Secretary of State of the Confederacy, and later the great "unreconstructed rebel," practiced the art of swaying people with his oratory. Here too, Benjamin Harvey Hill, United States Senator, debated such issues as State's Rights over a century ago.

PHI KAPPA HALL
1836

The Phi Kappa Literary Society, the arch rival of the Demosthenian Society, was housed in the building directly across the campus. Students belonged to either one or the other society and their rivalry was so serious that it often continued many years after college.

Although organized in 1820, funds were not raised for the building until sixteen years later. Alexander H. Stephens, one of the founders and later Vice-President of the Confederacy, was zealous in the campaign to secure the building funds. Other noted members of the society were Joseph Henry Lumpkin, the first Chief Justice of the Georgia Supreme Court, General Thomas R. R. Cobb, who codified the laws of the State of Georgia, and Henry W. Grady, noted Southern newspaper-man and editor of the Atlanta Constitution.

The second floor of the old *Phi Kappa Hall* holds the assembly room where debates are still held. Oratory was of such prime interest to antebellum students that they voluntarily spent each Saturday, sometimes far into the night, participating in these debates.

During the War Between the States when classes were suspended after the first two war years, Chancellor Lipscomb acted as caretaker of the buildings. He delivered the traditional commencement sermon in the Chapel to townspeople even though there were no students or graduates. Later, Federal troops were quartered in the college buildings and the *Phi Kappa Hall* was turned into the Commandant's Headquarters.

Portraits of honored members hang on the wall. They are, from left to right, Justice Joseph Henry Lumpkin, Henry W. Grady, General Robert E. Lee, and Howell Cobb II.

The first floor of the building now houses the private library of Ellis Merton Coulter, Professor Emeritus of History, noted author and authority on the Confederate States of America.

THE CHAPEL
1832

The Greek Revival influence was beginning to affect campus architecture when this chapel was built at a cost of $15,000. Religion was a vital part of student life. The tolling college bell brought sleepy-eyed students to morning prayer services, and again at twenty minutes after sunset they were summoned to evening vespers. This practice continued until after the War Between the States.

It was here that the commencement sermons were delivered each year to overflowing crowds.

PAINTING OF ST. PETER'S CATHEDRAL
CHAPEL

A large painting of St. Peter's Cathedral, mounted back of the stage of the Chapel, gives the impression of a continuation of the church. George Cook, the artist (1783-1857) and native of Maryland, married the widow of Asbury Hull, a well-known Athenian.

Measuring 17 feet by 23½ feet, and weighing a ton when mounted, it has been described as the largest framed oil painting in the world, as well as one of the most remarkable. It was given to the University in 1867 by Daniel Pratt, a distinguished Piedmont architect.

NEW COLLEGE
1832

The first *New College,* erected in 1822, burned in 1830 just at the time the college and the State Legislature were disagreeing over the merits of having a college. The trustees won a partial victory and funds were appropriated for the *New College* which was built at a cost of $12,349. Modern day pharmacy students, using the old classrooms, are generally unaware of the tremendous struggle the faculty experienced securing this building for their use.

The building has served as a dormitory and recitation hall.

LUSTRAT HOUSE
1847

As the college grew, a number of homes for professors were built around the campus quadrangle. From this vantage point, antebellum professors could better police the campus. Unmarried professors and tutors lived on various floors of the dormitories where they were "spy, policeman and judge." This was a distasteful assignment in those early times, for students were guided by a rigorous code of laws regulating every detail of their student life, and infractions were multitudinous.

The *Lustrat House,* one such professor's home, was named for Professor Joseph Lustrat whose family last occupied the house from 1904 until his death in 1927. He came to the University from France and was the head of the Romance Languages Department.

PAINTING OF ILAH DUNLAP LITTLE
LUSTRAT HOUSE

The family paintings and a collection of 18th and 19th century furniture, which belonged to Mrs. Little, are now in the *Lustrat House.*

Mrs. Little who bequeathed funds for the building of the Memorial Library was the daughter of a Macon, Georgia, plantation owner and merchant. Her first husband, Col. Leonidas A. Jordan of Milledgeville, was one of the largest plantation owners in Middle Georgia. Following his death, she became the wife of John Dozier Little, Speaker of the Georgia House of Representatives in 1898 and 1899.

LIVING ROOM
LUSTRAT HOUSE

A pair of antique French crystal-and-bronze chandeliers are hung in the double living rooms of the house. Below the painting of Samuel Scott Dunlap, Sr., father of Mrs. Little, is a rare French clock. The rosewood chairs, done in the style of John Belter, are a part of a set of Victorian furniture in the house. The lamp is Wedgewood.

COMMENCEMENT PROCESSION

Commencement day "before surrender" climaxed an exciting week in Athens. Every facility of the town was strained to provide hospitality for the crowds that made their annual pilgrimage to the village to see and hear what was going on. The cultured, the country folks, the "poor whites," the statesmen, the politicians, the young people, and the "dandies" were all there. Slaves came with their masters for it was a holiday for the Negroes as well. By 1828, only half the crowd could squeeze into the old Chapel, hastening the erection of the new building.

Declamations and the commencement sermon kept the tone of the occasion on a high plane. Music added to the festivities as well as picnic baskets full of chicken pies, ginger cakes, lemonade and watermelons.

After the War, commencement never regained its robust vitality. However, the Sheriff of the county still leads the procession dressed in a frock coat, red sash, wide-brimmed Southern Planter's hat, and carrying a sword, his symbol of office. This cherished custom has persisted ever since the first commencement when the Sheriff was asked to maintain order and lead the ten graduates up to the brush arbor in front of the unfinished *Old College* where they received the first degrees issued by the University.

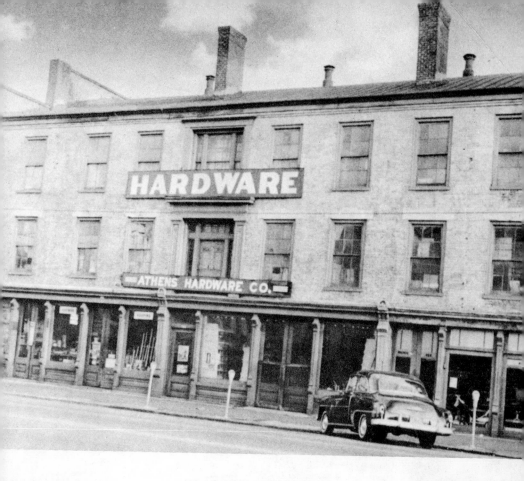

FRANKLIN HOTEL
1845
480 East Broad Street

Old *Franklin Hotel* was preceeded by Capt. John Cary's hotel which was built in 1805 when Athens had two stores, a flour mill, a common grist mill, a saw mill, a cake shop, grog shop, a blacksmith, and a tailor. By 1806 there were ten homes on the streets which had been laid out in 1804 by the University trustees for orderly growth of the village. It was at Cary's hotel that popular President Monroe was entertained on his tour of the South in 1819, the same year Florida was purchased from Spain and Alabama was admitted to the Union as the 22nd state.

Across Broad Street from the site of Carey's hotel stands the Athens Hardware Co., once the famous *Franklin Hotel* with an inviting three-tiered portico extending across the front. Doors to each upper level can still be seen behind the Hardware signs.

BRUMBY HOUSE
1818
343 Hancock Street

Most of the early homes of Athens were built in *Lickskillet,* an area bounded by Clayton, Jackson, Hoyt Streets, and the river, as was the *Brumby House*. It is now the oldest extant home built in Athens. Alonzo Church employed a New England contractor to build this Federal home, selling it after he became president of the University (1829-1859).

In 1835 the house was bought from President Church by the estate of Stephen W. Harris, and since then members of the Harris and Brumby families have occupied it. The Brumby's Drug Store became the scene of excitement when on a cold December day in 1896 it was lighted by electric lights with power supplied from the hydro plant on the Middle Oconee River. This was the beginning of electric lighting for the homes of Athens.

DOORWAY
HUBERT B. OWENS HOUSE
c. 1822
215 Rutherford Street

This nine-paneled door, below the segmented fan light, was rescued by Professor Owens from the *Reeves House* on Jackson Street, built in 1822, when it was torn down. Being too wide for modern homes, the door was split to form two doors for the present residence erected in 1941. The woodwork is of the Regency period.

ERWIN HOUSE
c. 1828
126 Dearing Street

John Addison Cobb, father of Howell and Thomas R. R., turned to Connecticut for the designer of this home which he built for his sister, Mildred, when she became the bride of William H. Jackson, son of Governor James Jackson. Mr. Jackson bequeathed a plot of ground to a tree. The plot, now fenced, is occupied by a descendant of the original "tree that owns itself."

Some years later, Mathus Ward, teacher of Natural History and Curator of the University Garden, the first botanical garden of the South, acquired the house. The gardens covered the adjoining hillside, which he filled with rare specimens such as the Upland Cypress and Ginkgo trees still standing beside the house. Around a lake formed by Tanyard Branch and along the garden paths he grew grapes from the Cape of Good Hope and a weeping willow tree started from a sprig which the French government sent from the tomb of Napoleon at St. Helena to William H. Crawford, American Legate to France.

The house is presently owned by Mr. and Mrs. Howell Cobb Erwin, Jr., the sixth generation nephew of John A. Cobb, the builder.

PORTRAIT OF HONORABLE HOWELL COBB
ERWIN HOUSE

The nameplate below the portrait bears the inscription: "Hon. Howell Cobb, Speaker of the House of Representatives of 31st Congress." He also served as Governor of Georgia, Secretary of the Treasury under President James Buchanan, and President of the Constitutional Convention of the Confederacy.

The Adamesque mantel with its sunburst pattern is typical of the period as well as the heart-of-pine floors, prized for their hardness.

ROSEWOOD PIANO
ERWIN HOUSE

This 1848 R. Nunns & Clark square, rosewood piano, made in New York, on<
longed to Hon. Howell Cobb. The French ormolu candelabra are cherished posse
of Mrs. Erwin, Jr.

GENERAL THOMAS R. R. COBB HOUSE
c. 1830
194 Prince Avenue

The Cobb family brought state and national fame to Athens. Their fine Classic homes still stand as reminders of these distinguished men. Standing far back from the street, this expansive house with its octagonal wings and facade, added by General Thomas Reeds Rootes Cobb, was once his home. It is now the parish house of St. Joseph's Roman Catholic Church.

Thomas R. R. Cobb took up law in his youth and in time became one of Georgia's most noted lawyers. He codified the laws of the state known as Cobb's Digest and was co-founder of the Lucy Cobb Institute, a private finishing school for girls. He was a member of the General Assembly of Georgia and wrote the Confederate Constitution. Later he served as Brigadier-General of the Confederate Army and was killed at the Battle of Fredericksburg,—ironically on the same hill where his mother's family lived and died.

GENERAL HOWELL COBB HOUSE
1835
698 Pope Street

To this stately house Howell Cobb brought his bride, Miss Mary Ann Lamar. In the years to come he was to bring her many honors, although it was her brother, John, who provided much of the means from his large plantation operations to sustain Howell and Mary during the General's years of devotion to his country's service.

During the great national debate preceding the War Between the States, Howell remained loyal to President James Buchanan who had appointed him his Secretary of the Treasury. In 1860 Howell finally spoke out in favor of secession and became president of the Constitutional Convention of the Confederate States of America. He later fought for the Confederacy.

This house was occupied for a time by Senator Pope Barrow.

ATHENS REGIONAL LIBRARY
1830
193 East Hancock Street

Busy Hancock Avenue was a quiet, tree-lined street when James Tinsley built this Federal home more than a half century before paving with Belgium blocks first appeared in Athens on several blocks of Broad Street. On hot days the contour of these cobble-stones can still be seen below the asphalt now covering them.

In time, the house became known as the Old Stern House. Like many homes standing in the path of a growing town, it lost caste and became a boarding house, a mortuary, and finally a rooming house before it was restored in 1949 as a much needed city library.

JAMES CAMAK HOUSE
MASONIC TEMPLE
1830
279 Meigs Street

This square brick building of the Federal period stands alone in its block as was the custom of all early homes of Athens. The year James Camak built this fine house, it took two months for the news of Bonaparte's escape from Elba to reach Athens, coming finally by stage from Augusta.

Albeit James Camak was professor of mathematics at the college from 1817-19, he did well in business. In 1834 a group of business men met in this house to organize the Georgia Railroad, the first railroad built in Georgia and the third such enterprise in the United States. Mr. Camak became the first president of the railroad as well as of the Branch Bank of the State of Georgia when it was organized in 1835. It was a milestone in Athens' history when the Georgia Railroad finally reached Carr's Hill overlooking the city in 1846.

Five generations of Camaks lived in this house before it was acquired by the Masonic Order in 1949.

ENTRY CAMAK HOUSE

Athens began, while still a village, to attract educational and cultural leaders of Georgia who built homes there to enjoy its social life. The *Camak House* was built facing the Jefferson Road and was at that time on the edge of the growing town. The ironwork was made locally for Athens had an ironworks and several brickworks as early as the 1840's.

Dr. Crawford W. Long focused national attention on Georgia when he discovered the beneficial use of sulphuric ether as an anesthetic, March 30, 1842. He was living in Jefferson, eighteen miles north of Athens, at the time, but spent most of his professional life in Athens. For this service to mankind, the State of Georgia nominated him for Statuary Hall in the nation's capital. Interestingly, the other nominee, Alexander H. Stephens, Vice-President of the Confederacy, had been Dr. Long's roommate at the University.

CRAWFORD W. LONG HOUSE
KAPPA PSI FRATERNITY HOUSE
c. 1830

GLOVER HOUSE
after 1830
225 Milledge Heights

The *Glover House* was built by Alonzo Church as his country retirement home and called *Homewood*. He lived in the house until his death in 1860. In 1863 it was sold to Frederick W. Lucas and later to the Carlton family.

The original wheat sheaf balustrade and heart-of-pine floors were preserved by Mrs. Zena T. Glover, the present owner, when she had the house restored.

MOSS-SIDE
1838
479 Cobb Street

Dr. William Lorenzo Moss, who discovered blood typing while doing research at Johns Hopkins Hospital, was born in this modest frame house. Working independently, two men—Dr. Moss in the United States, and the other in Austria—discovered blood typing simultaneously.

In the yard stands quaint "Old Grove school" where "Miss Jule" Moss kept school for her nieces and nephews, and later, the children of the neighbors, long before Athens opened its first public school in 1886. Miss Sarah Hunter Moss, one of the nieces, a sister of Dr. Moss, became so impressed with the importance of a broad education that she bequeathed funds to establish University of Georgia faculty postgraduate scholarships for study outside of the Southeast to combat provincialism.

This home was built by Hiram Hayes, and purchased in 1861 by the Moss family. The property is still owned by the Moss family.

STEPHEN UPSON HOUSE
1840
1022 Prince Avenue

For its "rigid adherence to the classic tradition and the purity of its line and fine proportions", — this house has been referred to as "pillared elegance."

Built as a plantation home by Dr. Leonidas Franklin, physician and teacher, it now stands behind six huge magnolia trees on busy Prince Avenue. This formal house boasts of silver doorknobs and covered keyholes, herringbone parquet floors of quarter-sawed oak bordered with inlays of mahogany and rosewood, doors and stairways of solid mahogany, and solid foot and a half thick brick walls. Rare trees, once part of an extensive formal garden, still shade the grounds.

PARLOR
UPSON HOUSE

Mr. and Mrs. Bradbury Poor Foss treasure the *Stephen Upson House,* which has been in Mrs. Foss's family for four generations. Mrs. Foss is the granddaughter of Mrs. Edwin King Lumpkin, founder of the first garden club in America.

Columns adorning the facade of the house provide the motif for the interior trim, fireplace, and doors of the house. The Vieux Paris vases beside the Federal, acorn mirror on the mantel are typical of the many precious art objects, outstanding furniture, oriental rugs, and rare first edition books in the house.

PARLOR
UPSON HOUSE

The *Stephen Upson House* contains four fine portraits of Mrs. Foss's forebears, **two** of which are shown here. Stephen Cumming Upson, her grandfather, was a trustee of Yale University. Upson County, Georgia, was named for him. The portrait of Esther Upson Cox was done in the late 1700's.

The lowboy once belonged to General Enoch Poor, a forebear of Mr. Foss, who was killed in the Revolutionary War Battle of Saratoga. The house boasts of many pre-Revolutionary pieces as well as some original Chippendale chairs.

NICHOLSON HOUSE
1825-1840
298 Hull Street

Thomas Wray desired a home near the campus, so he purchased an 1825 student dining-hall and transformed it into this elegant home in 1840. Into it he built a secret stair. A dry well outside provided cold storage for food.

By 1840, industry was on the upswing in Athens. It had three milliners, two mantua makers, the Athens Manufacturing Company, and the Georgia Factory which has been in continuous operation since 1828.

John W. Nicholson and William S. Grady, the father of Henry W. Grady, built the town's first gas works in 1852. Gas was made by burning pine knots. Poles for street lighting, erected from the Post Office on East Clayton to Franklin Street, were outfitted with lanterns. Business was going well for Mr. Nicholson when he took over the Wray home in 1867.

TREANOR HOUSE
c. 1840
1234 South Lumpkin Street

This fine house with its attenuated Gothic columns was once the home of John Addison Cobb and Sarah Robinson Rootes, parents of Howell and Thomas R. R. Cobb and Laura Cobb Rutherford. It was here that Mildred Lewis Rutherford, Laura's daughter, was born about 1860. She later became the director of the fashionable Lucy Cobb Institute.

"Miss Millie" also became one of the most famous of Georgian women. She reorganized the Athens Chapter of the United Daughters of the Confederacy. Touring the country as a speaker, she frequently appeared on the platform dressed in an antebellum gown defending the South's part in the War Between the States.

GOVERNOR WILSON LUMPKIN HOUSE
1842
South Campus

Classic homes were being built on the new streets of Athens when Governor Wilson Lumpkin decided he would build a home resembling the old mill-house at Cedar Shoals, one of the first buildings in Athens. He imported masons from England to construct the house at a cost of $11,000.

Governor Lumpkin was the father of Martha Atalanta Lumpkin Compton for whom Atlanta was first named Marthasville, and later Atlanta, when it became apparent the city would become more than a village. Why the "a" was dropped from Atalanta is not known.

Martha sold the house to the University in 1906, with the proviso that the house must remain intact or the land returned to her heirs.

(on opposite page)

Joseph Henry Lumpkin, First Chief Justice of the Supreme Court of Georgia and brother of Governor Wilson Lumpkin, built this pillared home on a fifty acre tract of land. The judge's law office stood near the corner of Prince and Pulaski Streets. Circuit sessions of the Supreme Court were held in the old frame building recently demolished. Here also this former student of the University with his son-in-law, Thomas R. R. Cobb, began to teach law students and in time their school was made a part of the University, named the Lumpkin Law School.

Sometime later, the house became the "Home School," an elementary school for girls, run for thirteen years by Madam Sophia and Miss Callie Sosnowski, two Polish noble-women. In 1919 the house was acquired by the Athens Woman's Club.

JOSEPH HENRY LUMPKIN HOUSE
ATHENS WOMAN'S CLUB
1842
248 Prince Avenue

ASBURY HULL HOUSE
1842

198 South Hull Street

Asbury Hull, Secretary and Treasurer of the University for almost half a century, was chairman of the organizational meeting of the Georgia Railroad and cashier of the newly organized Branch Bank of the State of Georgia in 1835.

Athens was well into the "good years" when this home was built. An old report says that "during its palmiest days," three turkey gobblers could be had for a dollar, beef was sold for three cents a pound, chicken at five cents, and taxes were twelve and one half cents per one hundred dollar valuation.

The house was once the home of Charles Snelling, University Chancellor, and later housed the Pi Kappa Alpha Fraternity.

ROSS CRANE HOUSE

SIGMA ALPHA EPSILON FRATERNITY HOUSE

1842

247 Pulaski Street

Ross Crane, a builder, erected this house some years before he designed the F i r s t Presbyterian Church in Athens. Old reports say the bricks for this dwelling were hauled by ox-cart from Augusta. It is one of the few remaining typical examples of a boxwood garden overhung by magnolia and crape-myrtle trees complementing the lovely Classic facade.

Greek letter fraternities first came to the campus in 1866. These organizations became rivals of the old Phi Kappa and Demosthenian Literary Societies for the active participation of the students.

HENRY W. GRADY HOUSE
1845

643 Prince Avenue

Henry W. Grady, known as the man "who loved a nation into peace," spent part of his boyhood in this Classic home built by General Robert Taylor. Through the editorial columns of the *Atlanta Constitution*, he urged the South to build a new economic future after the devastation of the War Between the States. The Grady School of Journalism of the University of Georgia is named for him. The thirteen Doric columns surrounding three sides of this house are said to represent the thirteen colonies bound together in a Union just as these columns are bound by the iron railing.

42

STEVENS THOMAS
HOUSE
Y.W.C.A. BUILDING
1848
347 Hancock Street

The *Stevens Thomas House* originally faced Pulaski Street, surrounded by an extensive garden. Col. Stevens Thomas came to Athens early in the 1800's where be became a "merchant prince." He married the daughter of Mrs. Lucy Carey, a friend of George and Martha Washington.

The year before Mr. Thomas built his fine home, the city government was changed from a three-man elected commission to an intendant with seven wardens with police powers. The town marshal had the duty of ringing the market bell notifying the people that fresh meat was available at Town Hall. He also had the duty of stopping marble playing on the sidewalk during the week and anywhere on Sunday. Vehicles were forbidden to cross the town's bridges at a pace faster than a walk.

PARLOR
STEVENS THOMAS HOUSE

The arch design of the brown marble mantel in the *Stevens Thomas House* was popular during the Victorian period. The Louis XIV ormolu clock on the mantel is typical of the Rococo period.

This massive, 18th
its flame grain and dr
wood, now in the *Ste*
from the *Camak Ho*
Chinese Rose Medal

THOMAS HOUSE

ry mahogany desk with
, faced with pecan
homas House, c a m e
is filled with rare old
'ith People china.

PARLOR CHANDELIER
STEVENS THOMAS HOUSE

The parlor chandelier in the *Stevens Thomas House* with its fleur-de-lis etched glass was recently given to the house by Mrs. Marion DuBose. It came from the Darwin home near Ware Shoals, South Carolina, and is believed to be about 150 years old.

MELL HOUSE
1848
897 South Milledge Avenue

Milledge Avenue had not yet been laid out when this home with its triple-cluster columns was erected by Lewis J. Lampkin on the corner of Jackson and Strong Streets. Colonel L. H. Charbonnier, Professor of Engineering, later occupied it before the house was sold to Reverend John Mell who had it moved and rebuilt on its present site.

COFER HOUSE
c. 1870
329 Dearing Street

Although built many years later, graceful attenuated-Gothic columns similar to those found on the *Mell* and *Treanor Houses* support the wide porch of the *Cofer House*. Built by C. Samuel P. Thurmond, a successful lawyer, this lovely house rests on a slight elevation surrounded by ancient oaks and English boxwoods. Its cupola is a rare feature in the Piedmont.

SLEDGE HOUSE
1853
749 Cobb Street

The 1850's was a boom era for Athens as well as all the South. The 1852 town population reached 3462 persons, white and Negro. Victorian architecture was beginning to take its place alongside the Classic Revival homes on the magnolia-lined streets when James A. Sledge built this scroll-saw Gothic house. Mr. Sledge was prospering as the editor of the *Southern Banner,* the forerunner of *The Banner-Herald.*

The house later became known as the *Cobb House,* for it was the home of Mrs. Lamar Cobb who became the first president of the Ladies Garden Club of Athens.

HALL
SLEDGE-COBB HOUSE

Cathedral doors of the *Sledge-Cobb House* furnish the motif for the woodwork trim throughout this house. The wood beneath the paint is solid walnut. The mantels in the house are made of cast iron, painted white. The interior walls are solid brick throughout, making it difficult to install modern conveniences.

FIRST PRESBYTERIAN CHURCH
1855
185 East Hancock Street

Mounted atop a cupola, a nine-foot wooden hand with the index finger pointing skyward reminded 19th century Athenians of less worldly matters. The cupola and hand were removed from the church, built by Ross Crane, when it was remodeled in 1902.

The cost of constructing the church in 1855 was $10,000.

INTERIOR
FIRST
PRESBYTERIAN
CHURCH

The original, tiny-slatted shutters have been removed from the windows of this old church. However, the pristine charm of its early appearance has been retained. Negro worshippers attended services here before the War Between the States, being seated in the balcony at the rear of the church.

A. P. DEARING HOUSE
KAPPA ALPHA THETA SORORITY HOUSE
1856

338 Milledge Avenue

Milledge Avenue had been opened up for settlement the year before William Dearing built this house of red bricks made in the Athens area. The outer walls are two feet thick resting on a brick foundation. The columns are also solid brick covered with fluted plaster. This house is considered one of the "most perfect examples of Grecian architecture in America." It remained in the Dearing family until it was acquired by the Kappa Alpha Theta Sorority in 1938.

PARLOR
A. P. DEARING HOUSE

A. P. Dearing had the mantels and woodwork of his home constructed of maple and fruit wood. The floor length windows emphasize the fourteen foot height of the ceilings.

Mrs. Howell Cobb Erwin, Sr., whose portrait hangs over the parlor mantel, is honored as the "grandmother" of the Athens chapter of Kappa Alpha Theta Sorority. Her husband is the grandson of General Howell Cobb.

THOMAS R. R. COBB SECRETARY
A. P. DEARING HOUSE

The massive mahogany, inlaid with rosewood, secretary in the parlor of the *A. P. Dearing House* once belonged to General Thomas R. R. Cobb, author of the Confederate Constitution. When opened, the pigeon holes display fine silver markers fashioned in Spencerian handwriting. Candles on the candlestands at the sides of the desk may well have given light to the General as he drafted the Constitution.

A. T. DEARING HOUSE

Modern Athens is still nurturing daughters proud of the Old South. These Kappa Alpha Theta Sorority sisters are wearing their "Old South Ball" gowns in preparation for the ball much as daughters of the Confederacy graced these same *Dearing House* steps a century ago.

The University became co-educational in 1918. The newly dedicated freshman dormitory was named for Miss Eve Creswell who was one of the first women to be admitted. She later became Dean of the School of Home Economics.

WILKINS HOUSE
c. 1860
387 South Milledge Avenue

Brothers A. P. and William Dearing both built their homes on Milledge Avenue; William built this Classic mansion. Its Corinthian columns reaching around three sides of the dwelling were added by the Wilkins.

William Dearing and John Nisbet built the Athens Factory in 1834. Being astute businessmen, they sold the slaves they used to operate the mill before they were freed and placed the gold receipts with the British Consulate for safekeeping. During the War the mill turned its entire operation to the making of Confederate uniforms. Later, the mill became widely known for its famous *Daisy Check* ginghams, which won the Gold Medal Award at the 1876 exposition in New Orleans. The factory is still in operation as a branch of Chicopee Manufacturing Co.

This third *Dearing House* was built by A. P. Dearing for his mother, Mrs. William Dearing. The plan and proportions are the same as that of the *Kappa Alpha Theta House* although slightly smaller and constructed of wood at Mrs. Dearing's request. The house has been in Mrs. DuBose's family since the 1890's. It has now been demolished.

LUCY COBB INSTITUTE
1858
200 block North Milledge Avenue

A daring article appeared in the *Athens Watchman* in early 1857, entitled *The Education of Our Girls,* signed by *Mother*. The article caught the eye of General T. R. R. Cobb, who at the time had several daughters at home. The author said, "girls have the same intellectual constitution as men and have the same right as men to intellectual cultural development."

General Cobb immediately set about raising funds to establish a school for girls. In 1858, the doors were opened to what was to become one of the South's most fashionable finishing schools for girls. The school was named in honor of Lucy, a daughter of General Cobb, who had recently succumbed to scarlet fever.

In later years, Miss Millie Rutherford and Mrs. Mary Ann Lipscomb, daughters of the writer of the article, who were also nieces of General Cobb, became directors of the school.

Intricate ironwork adorns the 100 foot veranda. Carefully protected daughters of Southern gentlemen were not allowed to wander beyond the magnolia trees in the front yard without a chaperon.

58

SENEY-STOVALL CHAPEL AT LUCY COBB INSTITUTE

1885

Milledge and Reese Streets

This octagonal brick building was a most welcome gift to the Institute. It seems students of a particular class were encouraged to write letters to philanthropists around the country asking for a chapel. A letter written by Miss Nellie G. Stovall to George I. Seney of New York enlisted his interst. The chapel he provided was therefore named for the two principals in this episode. It was dedicated in 1885.

UNIVERSITY
PRESIDENT'S HOUSE
1856
570 Prince Avenue

John Thomas Grant, a Virginian, built this outstanding Greek Revival residence with its 14 Corinthian columns extending around the three "sunny sides" of the structure. The Doric columns at the back of the house face a nine-acre garden where presidents of the University of Georgia and their wives have received thousands of guests since this became their official residence in 1949.

The formal boxwood, parterre garden fronting the house is surrounded by shrubbery and the traditional picket fence. The residence has been described by a leading expert on the Classic Revival Period Architecture and Landscape Architecture as a "veritable museum piece" because both the house and garden which complement each other are such fine, typical examples of this period of classic design.

EAST PARLOR
UNIVERSITY PRESIDENT'S HOUSE

Double parlors flanking the spacious central hallway in the *President's House* are adorned with thumb-print crystal chandeliers, ceiling medallions and deep cornices. The intricate fruit-and-floral friezes and the marble mantels were added later by Benjamin Harvey Hill when he acquired the house in 1876. A member of both the House and Senate in Washington, it is said Hill was able to persuade President Hayes to withdraw Federal occupation troops in 1877, thus ending military rule in Georgia and the Reconstruction Era.

The painting of the 18th century Roman Ruins from the school of Painini, which hangs over the drawing room mantel, is only one of the many precious art objects the University has placed in this historic home.

STAIRWAY
UNIVERSITY PRESIDENT'S HOUSE

The carved stairway with its octagonal newel post leads from the back of the wide central hallway in the *President's House* as did most of the stairways of the period.

HAMILTON HOUSE
ALPHA DELTA PI SORORITY HOUSE
1858
150 South Milledge Avenue

Although J. E. Hamilton had completed his home with its solid, foot-thick brick walls, eleven mantels, and solid mahogany trim, the ornamental ironwork trim had not yet arrived from England when outbreak of the War Between the States became im-minent. Fortunately, the precious cargo reached Philadelphia just in time to be loaded onto the last train to leave that city before traffic was closed because of the war. Mr. Hamilton is said to have been Georgia's first millionaire. The intricate Arabesque frieze and wide, light Saracenic arches supported by clustered columns must have been the pride of the owner when they were finally mounted. Even the bannister design adapts the Saracenic arch for its patterned beauty.

During the War, the Hamiltons housed many wounded and ill Confederate soldiers as did many of the homes in Athens.

HALL
HAMILTON HOUSE

The spacious entrance hall of the *Hamilton House* is typical of the inviting entrances of these antebellum homes. The wide door jamb shows the thickness of the walls.

NORTH PARLOR
HAMILTON HOUSE
The arched, marble man
tel and floral plasterwork
of the cornices in the
Hamilton House were
characteristic of a num-
ber of homes of the pe-
riod.

(on opposite page)

Thomas N. Hamilton, father of Mrs. A. P. Dearing, built this house with its striking, double-tiered portico. The iron bannister, identical with the Saracenic arch bannister of the *J. E. Hamilton House,* may have come in the same shipment from England. However, Athens had two foundries at that time where the design could have been duplicated by skilled workmen.

The Phinizy name has long been prominent in the affairs of Athens, Augusta, and Lexington, Georgia. Ferdinand Phinizy was an outstanding merchant, while Billups Phinizy, his son, was a leading hotelman. Hardiman & Phinizy was a well-known cotton firm. Mrs. Robert Segrest, who now cherishes this picturesque dwelling, is the granddaughter of Ferdinand Phinizy.

SEGREST HOUSE
1858
250 South Milledge Avenue

Double parlors flank the entrance h a l l of the *Segrest House.* This parlor was done in the Directoire style by a decorator from Philadelphia in 1898. The frieze was painted in oils on plaster. The walls are covered with rose silk damask in keeping with the rose and beige colored crystal tile of the fireplace which is decorated w i t h gold-leafed, embossed garlands, torches, and a winged cherub. The entire room is a fine example of its period.

SOUTH PARLOR

NORTH PARLOR
SEGREST HOUSE

The north parlor of the *Segrest House* is done in the Victorian manner with its plaster, garlanded frieze. The panels over the windows are tooled leather. The mantel set is precious Sevres. Mrs. Segrest has furnished the house in keeping with its period.

CHANDELIER
SEGREST HOUSE

The delicate ceiling medallion of acanthus leaves and rose garlands in the north parlor of *Segrest House* befits the hand-cut crystal chandelier which has never been converted from gas to electricity.

(on opposite page)

General Robert Taylor also built this house which has been known in recent times as the *Edwin King Lumpkin House.* Judge Lumpkin was a grandson of Joseph Henry Lumpkin, First Chief Justice of the Georgia Supreme Court.

It was in this house that Mary Bryan Thomas Lumpkin, the Judge's wife, called together twelve women on a frosty day in January, 1891, to organize the Ladies Garden Club of Athens, the first garden club in America. Although Mrs. Lumpkin was the mother of 13 children, of whom 9 grew to adulthood, she still found time to spend in her home garden which she "adored." It is said that Mrs. Lumpkin was too modest to accept the first presidency which went to Mrs. Lamar Cobb.

E. K. LUMPKIN HOUSE
c. 1859
793 Prince Avenue

GRILLWORK
E. K. LUMPKIN HOUSE

The grape leaf pattern of the ironwork of the *Lumpkin House* veranda forms a "lacy" frame for the Young Harris Methodist Church which now owns this historic *Lumpkin House.*

FOUNDER'S MEMORIAL GARDEN
1857
S. Lumpkin St.

In 1939, the National Council of State Garden Clubs officially recognized the Ladies Garden Club of Athens as the first such club in the nation. A Memorial Garden was built on the campus as a joint project of the Garden Club of Georgia and the Landscape Architecture Department of the University.

Below a boxwood garden area is a large sunken garden surrounded by a serpentine brick wall. Its statuary and pool were given as memorials by various garden clubs. The central figure here was presented to the garden by the National Council of State Garden Clubs in 1954, the 25th anniversary of the National Council of State Garden Clubs.

The residence in the background, adjoining the garden, is a restored 1857 home built as a professor's residence by the University. On the extreme left is the kitchen building, and to the right is the smokehouse.

The upper section of the garden was designed in the manner of Piedmont gardens of the period from 1820 to 1860. Such antebellum gardens, placed in front of the house for viewing from the portico, were divided by a central walk with either identical or matching patterns of boxwood beds and walks on each side. The picket fence was also traditional. The *Memorial Garden* features miniature boxwood beds outlining four of the state's products—a cotton boll, a watermelon, a peach and a Cherokee rose.

MEMORIAL GARDEN
S. Lumpkin Street

74

HUNNICUTT HOUSE
1865
325 North Milledge Avenue

John F. Phinizy built one of the few houses that the impoverished South could afford immediately after the war. In more recent times, the house has come to be known for the Hunnicutt family which still occupies it. John A. Hunnicutt was one of the organizers of the Athens Electric Railroad Company in 1894.

Soon after Reconstruction, Old Athens began to give way to a New Athens. The University broadened its curriculum to better meet the needs of the State. Progress was really afoot when a Mr. Snodgrass brought three pony-sized mules from Texas in 1885. He received permission to lay rails on several streets, and called his company *The Classic City Street Railway Company.* The service was excellent until Mr. Snodgrass grew homesick and sold out. A few short years later, the mules were succeeded by electric cars.

IRONWORK
HUNNICUTT HOUSE

The ironwork of the *Hunnicutt House* features a
stylized leaf pattern. The doves beside the baskets
of fruit are made of iron, but the bird on the awn-
ing rod is alive.

CARITHERS HOUSE
ALPHA GAMMA DELTA SORORITY HOUSE
1890's
530 South Milledge Avenue

The *Carithers House* with its grand design suited the mood of the prospering end of the century. Americans had attended the Chicago World's Fair in 1893 and liked the architecture they saw there. This Neo-Classic Carithers residence is typical of the Fair's influence.

The stirrings of Modern Times were being felt in Athens. The mayor had appointed the nation's first City Board of Health in 1873. The first telephone service had come to the burgeoning town in 1882 with 36 subscribers. In the 1890's, electric cars raced over the city tracks at an alarming speed of eight miles an hour. Athens was well on its way to becoming the sixth largest inland cotton port in the world. A contingent of United States troops, encamped on Hill Street, marched over muddy streets in 1898, hastening the first extensive paving of the city streets that year. By the end of the century Athens had a modern department store, a real water works, and a population of over 10,000. The old University town was expanding in every direction.

ORNAMENTAL FRIEZE
CARITHERS HOUSE

This Neo-Classic house made generous use of all the Grecian decorative details, including Ionic columns, garlands, balustrades, dentiled cornices and the stylized acanthus leaves on the decorative frieze.

INTERIOR
CARITHERS HOUSE

The interior of the *Carithers House* is as arresting as the exterior with its grand entrance hall paneled in solid walnut. The overmantel in the drawing room repeats the decorative features of the exterior of the house.

The rosewood turn-about seat, covered with blue damask, is in keeping with the Victorian era.

STAIRWAY
CARITHERS HOUSE

The stained glass window on the stair landing of the *Carithers House* was also characteristic of the Victorian era.

CHARLES PHINIZY HOUSE
DELTA ZETA SORORITY HOUSE
c. 1900
397 South Milledge Avenue

To this house Charles Phinizy brought his bride at the dawn of the 20th century. Many of the fine old homes of Athens such as this dwelling, now treasured by the Delta Zeta Sorority, have been preserved by the sororities and fraternities of the University.

THE MICHAEL HOUSE
1902
596 Prince Avenue

A no more truly Classic home was built in all of Athens than this turn of the century mansion situated between the regal *Grady House* and the princely *President's House*. The Michael family carried over into the new century the best of the last when Simon and Moses G. Michael built twin houses on Prince Avenue. This home remains, a tribute to the family that gave Athens its first modern department store in 1882.

KAPPA DELTA HOUSE
1923
1084 Prince Avenue

The *Kappa Delta House* was designed for James White, Jr., by Neel Reid, Atlanta's outstanding young architect just before his untimely death. The library is paneled in virgin pine from Alabama with boards two inches thick. The dwelling is one of the first homes to be so paneled in Georgia.

The house typifies the continued 20th century loyalty of Athenians to the Classic in architecture which has gained for them the right to call themselves the "Classic City of the South."

Thus the shadows of a gracious and proud 19th century reach into modern day Athens where rich memories linger in the old University halls and homes of tall columns and iron lace.

ADDENDUM

Since this book was first published in 1964 changes of ownership, of use, and even of location, as well as the unearthing of additional historical data, have outdated some of the information presented in these pages. The most important of these are:

Franklin Hotel *(Page 19)*. When the Athens Hardware Co. moved to another site, the old structure was bought by the Athens—Clarke Heritage Foundation in order to ensure its preservation. It is once again privately owned.

Brumby House *(Page 20)*. Now believed to have been constructed in 1818. When it was threatened by the extension of the downtown business district, Athens' oldest house was moved to a new site at 280 E. Dougherty Street and restored in 1971 through the joint efforts of the City of Athens and the Athens—Clarke Heritage Foundation. Now owned by the former and operated by the latter as the Athens Welcome Center, it is officially (and correctly) known as the Church—Waddel—Brumby House.

Erwin House *(Page 22)*. The given name of the second owner was Ma*l*thus. As the builder never occupied the house, it should be identified as the Jackson—Ward—Erwin House.

General Thomas R. R. Cobb House *(Page 25)*. Built for *Charles G. McKinley,* originally of Oglethorpe County and later a lawyer in Newnan, whose niece Mary McKinley later became the bride of Howell Cobb, Jr. As Mr. McKinley had lived in an adjoining house until 1837 *(see page 39),* this house probably was erected in the period *1835-37.* In 1842 it was bought by Joseph Henry Lumpkin "of Oglethorpe County" as a home for his daughter Marian. As married women could not then own property, the deed was made to her husband T. R. R. Cobb. The octagonal wings are believed to have been added *circa* 1854. Should be identified as the McKinley—T. R. R. Cobb House.

Athens Regional Library *(Page 27)*. Since the library moved to newer quarters several years ago, this structure has been used by Clarke County for offices. Should be identified as the Tinsley—Stern House.

Crawford W. Long House *(Page 30)*. Demolished. Site now devoted to a parking lot.

Glover House *(Page 31)*. Now the residence of Mr. and Mrs. Yancey M. Robertson. Should be identified as *Homewood* / The Church—Iucas—Carlton—Glover—Robertson House.

Upson House *(Pages 33-35)*. Acquired by the First National Bank after the deaths of Mr. and Mrs. Foss. Its original character has been preserved in the conversion from residential to banking purposes. Should be identified as the Franklin—Upson—Foss House / First National Bank Branch.

Joseph Henry Lumpkin House *(Pages 38-39)*. Built for *Charles G. McKinley* prior to 1837. In that year he sold it to Jesse Robinson, who in turn sold it in 1842 to John B. Lamar, brother of Mrs. Howell Cobb. It was bought in 1843 by Joseph Henry Lumpkin, who probably added the handsome columned facade, and subsequently it became the residence of banker and railroad president A. K. Childs. It is now owned by the Athens Woman's Club, the Georgia Bar Association, and the Alumni of the Lumpkin Law School at the University of Georgia, which are restoring it as a meeting place. Might properly be referred to as The Joseph Henry Lumpkin Center / The McKinley—Lumpkin—Childs House.

Henry W. Grady House *(Page 42)*. Now more accurately known as The Taylor—Grady House, it is owned by the City of Athens and leased to the Junior Assembly for use as an entertainment center.

Segrest (Hamilton) House *(Pages 66-69)*. Now owned by the Phi Mu Sorority. Should be identified as the Hamilton—Phinizy—Segrest House.

Charles Phinizy House *(Page 81)*. Delta Zeta having moved to other quarters, this is now a fraternity house. (The original owner was a son of Ferdinand Phinizy and a half-brother of Billups Phinizy, successive owners of the house depicted on pages 66-69.)

Kappa Delta House *(Page 83)*. Now owned by Delta Tau Delta Fraternity. Should be identified as Delta Tau Delta / The James White, Jr. House.

The author expresses appreciation to these persons for assistance in obtaining the data used here: Mrs. Homer Cooper, Mrs. Ed Downs, Mrs. William Tate, and William B. Williford.